Joke Books

by Judy A. Winter

Consulting Editor: Gail Saunders-Smith, PhD

CAPSTONE PRESS
a capstone imprint

Pebble Books are published by Capstone Press,
151 Good Counsel Drive, P.O. Box 669, Mankato, Minnesota 56002.
www.capstonepub.com

Books published by Capstone Press are manufactured with paper
containing at least 10 percent post-consumer waste.

Library of Congress Cataloging-in-Publication Data
Winter, Judy A., 1952–
  Jokes about sports / by Judy A. Winter.
     p. cm. — (Pebble books. Joke books)
  Includes bibliographical references.
  Summary: "Simple text and photographs present jokes about sports"—Provided
by publisher.
  ISBN 978-1-4296-5270-4 (library binding)
  1. Sports—Juvenile humor. I. Title. II. Series.
  PN6231.S65W56 2011
  818'.602—dc22   2010029080

Editorial Credits
Gillia Olson, editor; Gene Bentdahl, designer; Sarah Schuette, studio specialist;
    Marcy Morin, studio scheduler; Laura Manthe, production specialist

Photo Credits
Barbara O'Brien, cover (chicken), 14 (chicken), 20 (dog); Capstone Press/Karon
Dubke, cover (nose and boy), 4, 6, 8, 10, 12, 14 (crate), 16, 18 (nose), 20 (gloves), 22;
Shutterstock/Khromov Alexey, 18 (field)

Note to Parents and Teachers

The Joke Books set supports English language arts standards related
to reading a wide range of print for personal fulfillment. Early readers
may need assistance to read some of the words and to use the Table of
Contents, Read More, and Internet Sites sections of this book.

Printed in the United States of America in North Mankato, Minnesota.
092010   005933CGS11

Table of Contents

4

Where do baseball catchers sit at lunch?
Behind the plate.

Why are baseball games at night?
Because bats sleep during the day.

Why did the football coach go to the bank?

He wanted his quarter back.

How do football players stay cool?

They stand close to their fans.

Which football player wears the biggest helmet? **The one with the biggest head.**

Which insect doesn't play well in football? **The fumble bee.**

Why do basketball players like cookies?
Because they dunk them.

What do you call a pig that plays basketball?
A ball hog.

What is a cheerleader's favorite color?

Yeller.

What is a cheerleader's favorite drink?

Rootbeer.

Why did the chicken get a penalty?
For fowl play!

How do hens cheer for their team?
They egg them on!

Why did the golfer wear two pairs of pants?

In case he got a hole in one.

Why was the computer so good at golf?

Because it had a hard drive.

Why wasn't the nose
on the soccer team?
It didn't get picked.

Why did the soccer ball
quit the team?
**It was tired of getting
kicked around.**

Why didn't the dog want to play baseball?

It's a boxer.

What do they call a boxer who gets knocked out?

A sore loser.

Why can't Cinderella play soccer?

She always runs away from the ball.

Why is Cinderella a poor basketball player?

She has a pumpkin for a coach.

Read More

Rosenberg, Pam. *Sports Jokes.* Mankato, Minn.: The Child's World, 2010.

Thornley, Stew. *Sports Jokes to Tickle Your Funny Bone.* Funny Bone Jokes. Berkeley Heights, N.J.: Enslow Publishers, 2010.

Internet Sites

FactHound offers a safe, fun way to find Internet sites related to this book. All of the sites on FactHound have been researched by our staff.

Here's all you do:

Visit *www.facthound.com*

Type in this code: 9781429652704

Super-cool stuff! Check out projects, games and lots more at **www.capstonekids.com**

Word Count: 236   **Grade:** 1
Early-Intervention Level: 20